Other books in the series:
The Crazy World of Birdwatching (Peter Rigby)
The Crazy World of Gardening (Bill Stott)
The Crazy World of Golf (Mike Scott)
The Crazy World of Jogging (David Pye)
The Crazy World of Love (Roland Fiddy)
The Crazy World of Marriage (Bill Stott)
The Crazy World of Music (Bill Stott)
The·Crazy World of Photography (Bill Stott)
The Crazy World of Sailing (Peter Rigby)
The Crazy World of Sex (David Pye)
The Crazy World of Skiing (Craig Peterson & Jerry Emerson)
The Crazy World of Tennis (Peter Rigby)

Published in Great Britain in 1988 by Exley Publications Ltd,
16 Chalk Hill, Watford, Herts WD1 4BN, United Kingdom.

Copyright © Bill Stott, 1988

ISBN 1-85015-110-5

Printed and bound in Hungary.

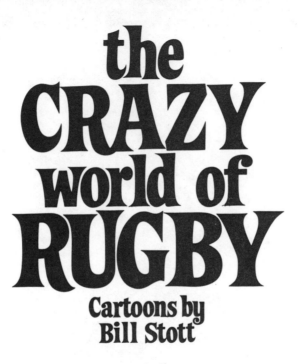

the CRAZY world of RUGBY

Cartoons by Bill Stott

EXLEY

"I saw that – you swallowed my whistle!"

"School rugby? It's done wonders for his character but not a lot for his teeth."

"Not releasing the ball ref? He <u>can't</u> release the ball."

"And leave their No.3 alone. He once got sent off for eating a spectator's dog."

"We need a new physio – he's using air freshener on my knee again ..."

"<u>How</u> many seasons since you played?"

"*Your try? Oh, you must have passed out quicker than I thought – it was disallowed.*"

"*The ball! I caught the ball!*"

"This is a sending-off offence, you know!"

"O.K. lightnin' release the ball!"

"Actually, he was hoping you'd send him off then he could go home and watch the international ..."

"Oh, ha, ha, very funny ..."

"It's not my fault. Can I help having an overprotective mother?"

"Wait."

"*I think I lost a lens.*"

"French referees usually have some quirky ideas about rule interpretation."

"Then Daddy shouted 'Up lads and at 'em', bopped their No.3 in the eye and got sent off."

"*Gaynor was wondering ... considering that I sometimes play for the ladies darts team, whether we'd mind if ...*"

"Lovely run – beautiful dummy, but you can't score tries with their number seven's boot ..."

"Did I stick my thumb in his eye? Certainly not..."

"... it was my finger."

"You can't have your ball back till you say sorry for pushing me over."

"That? – It's the ref's car. . . ."

"That? That's our star player – he gets too excited if we let him out too early ..."

"It's some sort of Australian joke ..."

"You know the old rugby maxim about no matter how rough and vindictive the game might have been, it's always forgotten in the bar?"

"Well?"

"Well, it's not true."

"When you said your friend was a hooker with a broken nose, I thought ..."

"Aaaagh! I'm stamping on my own hand!"

"*Rugby runs in his family. His auntie was a fine hooker.*"

"So I said to her – you wouldn't love me if I didn't play rugby on Sunday and roll home full of beer would you – she said yes!"

Rule 528: *"A good big 'un always beats..."*

"...a good little 'un."

"Men versus women? You don't stand a T^{H}U^N$_K$."

"*It works out at 26 sandwiches each, but my Terry likes his all at once …*"

"Stiff-arm tackle Malcolm when his mum's watching at your peril ..."

"*No.3 – stop telling jokes!*"

"Great kick – now do it with the ball."

"You think they **play** badly? Wait till you hear them sing!"

"There he was – way offside, so I naturally looked around for you - to draw your attention to the infringemet. You were nowhere to be seen."

"*So I floored him.*"

"For heaven's sake – what now?"

"Let's find the bung and let him down."

"He once had a county trial. They found him guilty."

"Go on Ref, don't call it off. Our forwards hate it too firm..."

"We can't find your teeth, but here are a few nobody claimed last week."

"*What do you mean, I'll look better with all my teeth in? This is all there are!*"

"*Teeth, glasses, hairpiece – sure you've taken everything off?*"

"*Chauvinist? Don't be silly – shut up and give us a kiss …*"

"Don't worry about there being anything wasted, our No. 5 will clear up for you ..."

"I've warned you about eating curry before a match!"

"I can't find the first aid box anywhere, so I'll bring him round with this bucket of wa ..."

"Nice try – no ball – but nice try!"

"*Rugby is <u>not</u> violent. I'll belt the next bloke who says it is!*"

"Great horned tortoiseshell or not – kick the ball!"

"*You can stop looking for a doctor in the crowd – it was his own who did it!*"

"I warned you about talking back to this referee, didn't I?"

"You're a very lucky man – not yet 20 and already invited to the President's brawl …"

"There are uncompromising players, dirty players, and Trevor."

"*You fool Qwrzgl, I told you to select a landing site where there were wars going on!*"

"Lousy kicker, but an absolute whizz at building the little mud towers the ball goes on."

"O.K. – I've got him …"

"*After a rugby match, there are no winners and losers, just drunks.*"

"When you're 6'6" and 300lbs, no one minds if you wear a shower cap."

"He's charged with insulting the referee and throwing the opposing team and two police officers into the canal."

"Did you win, then?"

"*Two-and-a-half minutes … that's some Gary Owen!*"

"Sorry, I didn't recognize you without your gumshield."

"Yes I did collapse the scrum. So would you if their No.3 kept asking you what aftershave you used."

"*He was hoping to turn out for the vets this week, but he fell off a bar stool.*"

"Go on – he called you a rude name – then what?"

"Hang on ref – be right with you ..."

"Well played – whoever you are!"

"Is your No.3 just a bit overweight, or am I playing against a bearded, pregnant lady?"

"*Get that dog into a shirt and a pair of shorts and we're in with a chance.*"

"*Just think – we go through this every week because some silly little public schoolboy picked up the ball and ran with it!*"

"Bloody hell! He's picked his missus again!"

"*I hate rugby, but I <u>love</u> rolling in mud.*"

"There! He'll have to stop – Rule 198, subsection (B), paragraph 4 'The corner flag shall at no time be used for anything other than marking a corner'!"

"He's just like his car – big, flashy and nowhere near as fast as he looks."

"Foul, Ref."

"Actually, I have it on good authority that he doesn't have a boy at the school. He just likes shouting at young people."

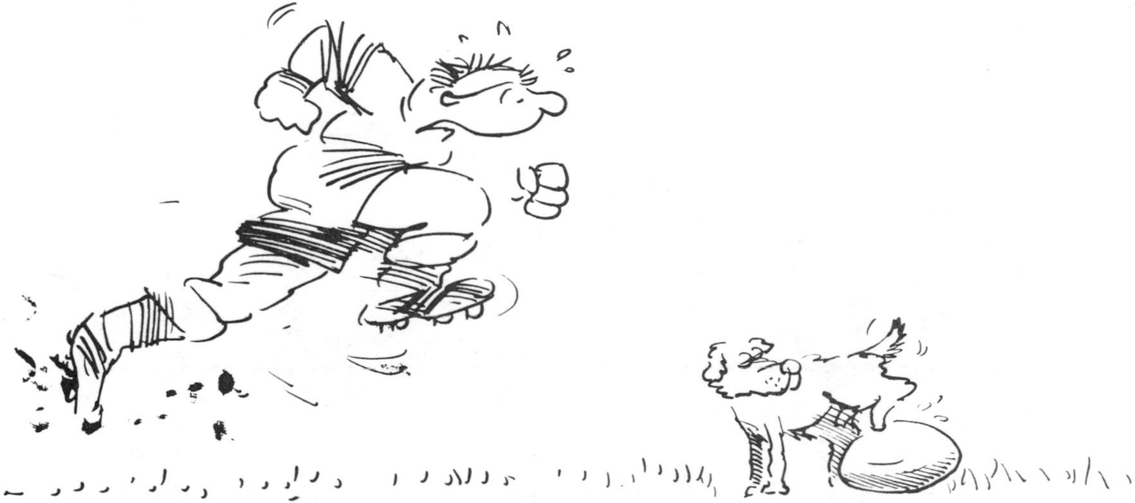

"Ooh look! A rainbow!"

"And in the fifth team, youth and maturity are united by one common factor – total lack of ability!"

Other books in the "Crazy World" series:

The Crazy World of Birdwatching. £3.99. By Peter Rigby. Over eighty cartoons on the strange antics of the twitcher brigade. One of our most popular pastimes, this will be a natural gift for any birdwatcher.

The Crazy World of Gardening. £3.99. By Bill Stott. The perfect present for anyone who has ever wrestled with a lawnmower that won't start, over-watered a pot plant or been assaulted by a rose bush from behind.

The Crazy World of Golf. £3.99. By Mike Scott. Over eighty hilarious cartoons show the fanatic golfer in his (or her) every absurdity. What really goes on out on the course, and the golfer's life when not playing are chronicled in loving detail.

The Crazy World of The Handyman. £3.99. By Roland Fiddy. This book is a must for anyone who has ever hung *one* length of wallpaper upside down or drilled through an electric cable. A gift for anyone who has ever tried to "do it yourself" and failed!

The Crazy World of Jogging. £3.99. By David Pye. An ideal present for all those who find themselves running early in the morning in the rain and wondering why they're there. They will find their reasons, their foibles and a lot of laughs in this collection.

The Crazy World of Love. £3.99. By Roland Fiddy. This funny yet tender collection covers every aspect of love from its first joys to its dying embers. An ideal gift for lovers of all ages to share with each other.

The Crazy World of Marriage. £3.99. By Bill Stott. The battle of the sexes in close-up from the altar to the grave, in public and in private, in and out of bed. See your friends, your enemies (and possibly yourselves?) as never before!

The Crazy World of Music. £3.99. By Bill Stott. This upbeat collection will delight music-lovers of all ages. From Beethoven to Wagner and from star conductor to the humblest orchestra member, everyone – even the tone-deaf – will enjoy their absurdities.

The Crazy World of Photography. £3.99. By Bill Stott. Everyone who owns a camera, be it a Box Brownie or the latest Pentax, will find something to laugh at in this superb collection. The absurdities of the camera freak will delight your whole family.

The Crazy World of Sailing. £3.99. By Peter Rigby. The perfect present for anyone who has ever messed about in boats, gone pea-green in a storm or been stuck in the doldrums.

The Crazy World of Sex. £3.99. By David Pye. A light-hearted look at the absurdities and weaker moments of human passion – the turn-ons and the turn-offs. Very funny and in (reasonably) good taste.

The Crazy World of Skiing. £3.99. By Craig Peterson and Jerry Emerson. Covering almost every possible (and impossible) experience on the slopes, this is an ideal present for anyone who has ever strapped on skis – and instantly fallen over. "A riotous suggestion ... very funny and very original." (The Good Book Guide)

The Crazy World of Tennis. £3.99. By Peter Rigby. Would-be Pat Cashes and Chris Everts watch out.... This brilliant collection will pinpoint their pretensions and poses. Whether you play yourself or only watch on TV, this will amuse and entertain you!